15 Easy-to-Read
Mini-Book Plays

BY SHERYL ANN CRAWFORD AND NANCY I. SANDERS

SCHOLASTIC
PROFESSIONAL BOOKS

New York • Toronto • London • Auckland • Sydney
Mexico City • New Delhi • Hong Kong • Buenos Aires

We would like to thank our editor, Deborah Schecter, for
her encouragement and professional guidance with each
book we write. Thanks, Deborah, for reading our plays on
the way home on the train—and laughing out loud!

—Sheryl and Nancy

Cover design by Susan Kass

Cover and interior illustrations on pages 15–64 by Anne Kennedy

Interior illustrations on pages 6–14 by James Graham Hale

Interior design by Sydney Wright

ISBN: 0-439-20155-1

Contents

Welcome!

Children love to giggle, and laughter is commonly known as good medicine for souls young and old. The 15 mini-book plays you'll find in these pages blend learning and laughter by introducing funny characters and silly situations—while at the same time building emergent reading skills and curriculum concepts!

We've grouped the reproducible mini-book plays in this collection into three familiar themes: Nutty Nature, Silly School Days, and Funny Fairy Tales and Nursery Rhymes. As children experience these plays in the classroom, they'll count to 100 as ants escape from an ant farm and march back in, they'll learn good manners from little monsters in school, and they'll practice phonics skills as silly bears create havoc at Goldilocks' house! These plays teach important early concepts and encourage children to become more confident readers.

Fun and easy extension activities are also included for each play, beginning on page 6. You can use these cross-curricular activities to reinforce concepts introduced in the plays and to support those that you teach.

Children might make stick puppets to perform the plays, or make simple costumes to wear as they act out the plays in front of the class. They might read the play books aloud in small groups, or you might divide the class so that small groups participate in choral reading. However you approach the task, we hope these play books make your class laugh and giggle as much as we did writing them, and that they will help keep children learning and growing as emergent readers!

—Sheryl Ann Crawford and Nancy I. Sanders

How to Make the Mini-Play Books

1. Make two-sided copies of the mini-play book pages.

✴ Start by making a photocopy of the first page of the mini-play book (cover and page 4). Position the cover in the upper left-hand corner of the copier's platen glass.

✴ Place this copy into the paper tray blank-side up.

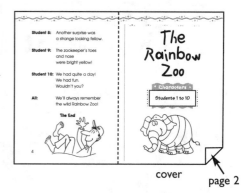

cover page 2

Check to be sure that the cover is in the upper left-hand corner of the tray. Then place the second page of the mini-play book (pages 2 and 3) on the platen glass with page 2 in the lower left-hand corner.

✴ If the play has 8 pages, repeat this process with pages 6 and 7 and pages 5 and 8.

(If your copier has a two-sided function and you would like to make copies using this feature, remove the mini-play book pages from the book.)

Regardless of how you make the two-sided copies, you may need to experiment to be sure the pages are aligned properly, and that page 2 appears directly behind page 1.

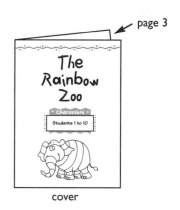

page 3

cover

2. Model for children how to assemble the books.

For a 4-page mini-play book, simply fold the cover and page 4 in half along the dotted line, keeping the fold to the left.

For an 8-page mini-play book:

✴ Fold the cover page and page 4 and pages 5 to 8 in half along the dotted lines, keeping the folds to the left side.

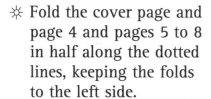

page 3 page 7

cover page 5

✴ Place the cover page to page 4 in front of pages 5 to 8.

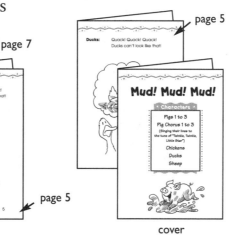

page 5

cover

✴ Check to be sure that the pages are in the proper order, and then staple them together along the book's spine.

complete book

Curriculum Connections

Nutty Nature

Literature Links

Animals Born Alive and Well by Ruth Heller (Paper Star, 1999). Nonfiction, rhyming text explains how baby animals are born.

Chickens Aren't the Only Ones by Ruth Heller (Paper Star, 1999). Explores the world of all sorts of hatching eggs.

Egg Crack-Up   **ART & SCIENCE**

Flip the Flaps

Help children make a flap book comparing the order of events in the life cycles of birds and mammals (explain that birds hatch from eggs, but mammals don't). Here's how:

☼ Make a flap book for each student by holding two pieces of white paper together vertically, as shown. Fold in half and staple across the fold. Lift all but the bottom sheet and cut to divide into two sets of flaps.

☼ On the first left flap of the front, have students draw a picture of an egg. On the right flap of the front, have students draw a picture of a baby mammal (cat, dog, bear, and so on). Tell students to label each picture.

☼ On the second page, have children draw a picture of each animal under the corresponding flap (the egg begins to hatch, the mammal gets bigger).

☼ On the third page, have children draw a picture of a bird and a full-grown mammal.

egg

2 sheets   fold   staple

Don't cut bottom page

Mud! Mud! Mud!

Barnyard Glyphs

Pigs love to roll in the mud! What do children like to do? Help them make barnyard glyphs to represent and organize information about their preferences (*glyphs* are symbolic representations of verbal ideas). Copy the legend below onto chart paper and discuss as a group what each symbol means. Then provide crayons and paper so children can create their own glyphs. When children are finished, they can "talk through" their glyphs to the group, explaining what each symbol means.

Literature Links

Mud by Mary Lyn Ray and Lauren Stringer (Harcourt Brace, 1996). A ground-level look at the joys of mud.

Pigs in the Mud in the Middle of the Rud by Lynn Plourde and John Schoenherr (Scholastic, 1992). A rhythmic, rhyming, muddy adventure!

Legend

1 Kind of Barn

Square-shaped red barn	Rectangle-shaped red barn
I'd rather play at a friend's home.	I'd rather play at home.

2 Color of Roof

Black roof	Brown roof	Red roof
I'd rather play in the grass.	I'd rather play in the snow.	I'd rather play in a lake.

3 Number of Windows

1 window	2 windows	3 windows
I'd rather eat pizza.	I'd rather eat dessert.	I'd rather eat something else.

4 Kind of Silo

Silo with dots	Silo with stripes
I like sports.	I don't like sports.

5 Color of Hay Bale

Green hay bale	Yellow hay bale
I like summer most of all.	I don't like summer most of all.

6 Kind of Animal

Pig	Chicken	Duck	Sheep
I like to play video games.	I like to play board games.	I like to play outdoor games.	I like to play different games.

Time to Get Dressed   MATH

Sorting Autumn Leaves

Explore concepts of shape and color while classifying autumn leaves:

☀ Use yellow, brown, green, red, and orange construction paper to create a pile of leaves in several different shapes. (Use all colors for each shape, so that within each group of same-shape leaves there are a variety of colors.)

☀ Share the pile during circle time and discuss classification and attributes. Invite children to think of ways to sort the leaves (by color, shape, size, and so on). Mix up the pile again.

☀ Post three large sheets of craft paper on the wall and draw simple brown "trunks" on each. Glue one kind of leaf to each trunk, so that each tree will have a different shape leaf. Children can use glue sticks to create autumn trees, sorting by shape as they go. (Point out that each tree grows a different shape leaf.)

Lullaby for Bear   SCIENCE

Animals in Winter Collaborative Book

Discuss the different things animals do when cold winter weather arrives and food is harder to find. Some animals migrate (geese, ladybugs, bats, salmon, caribou, and butterflies), or move to a warmer area to find food and shelter. Others hibernate (bears, groundhogs, snakes), or fall into a deep, sleep-like state. Other animals have characteristics that help them survive in the cold (polar bears have thick fur, dogs and cats are house pets). Let children draw an animal of their choice. Sort their pictures into a collaborative classroom book with three sections: We Hibernate, We Migrate, and We Stay Home. Bind the pages together into a classroom book.

A Buzzy Day

Counting Bees

Reinforce counting skills with an interactive garden game:

☼ Make ten flowers by stapling colorful paper petals around a paper plate. Use a hot glue gun (adult only) to attach a craft stick or dowel rod for a sturdy stem. Put a different number of "dot" (1-inch round) stickers in the center of each paper plate so that the numbers one to ten are represented.

☼ Make a copy of the ten bee patterns (below), cut them out, and glue each bee to a spring-type clothespin.

☼ To play the game, give flowers to half of the group and bees to the other half. The object of the game is for children to find their matching bee or flower.

☼ When a match is made, children clip the bee to its flower. When everyone has found a match, challenge children to line up in order!

Literature Links

The Bee Tree by Patricia Polacco (Philomel, 1993). Honeybees go on a colorful garden adventure.

The Honey Makers by Gail Gibbons (William Morrow, 1997). A nonfiction look at how bees make honey.

Literature Links

Animals Brightly Colored by Phyllis Limbacher Tildes (Charlesbridge, 1998). Riddles and colorful visual clues let readers guess the identities of seven animals, each a different color.

Brown Bear, Brown Bear, What Do You See? by Eric Carle and Bill Martin Jr. (Henry Holt & Co., 1996). Repetitive, rhyming question-and-answer text features animals of all colors.

The Rainbow Zoo   ART

Rainbow Animals

Set out different colors of clay or play dough and brainstorm which animals children might make with each color (for instance, for brown: bear, dog, or worm). Assign a small group of children to each color and give each group a sign that corresponds to their color: "Red Zoo," "Blue Zoo," and so on. Invite children to create a group of animals that might come in that color. When children are finished, they can look at other groups' zoos and talk about them.

Literature Links

The Hungry Monster by Phyllis Root and Sue Heap (Candlewick, 1998). A monster from outer space lands on Earth and eats everything in sight!

Monster Manners: A Guide to Monster Etiquette by Bethany Roberts and Andrew Glass (Houghton Mifflin, 1997). Three young monsters show their best and worst behavior.

Monster Rules   SOCIAL STUDIES

Good Little Monster Awards

Encourage children to be on the lookout for class-mates who are using good manners. When a child spots someone, he or she can fill out a "Good Little Monster" badge (see pattern, right) and present it to that child. (Use safety pins to attach the badges to children's clothing.) These awards will encourage children to smile, be polite, and say "please" and "thank you!"

Good Little Monster
Award

_____
name

100 Ants
MATH

Skip-Counting Strips

Build the concept of skip-counting by tens by creating a set of math manipulatives. Help each child cut an 8 1/2- by 11-inch sheet of light-colored construction paper (width-wise) into ten strips. Let children make ten thumbprints on each strip using water-soluble ink stamp pads. Children can use their sets of manipulatives to practice skip-counting by 10s to 100 (and more!) or to "act out" and solve addition and subtraction word problems, such as:

☼ If 40 ants marched to the picnic and 20 ants joined them, how many ants were at the picnic?

☼ If 100 ants ate a watermelon and 30 ants carried away the seeds to the trash can, how many ants were left?

☼ If half of 100 ants ate peaches and the other half ate brownies, how many ants ate brownies?

Literature Links

The Ant Bully by John Nickle (Scholastic, 1999). A boy is shrunk to ant-size and gains a new perspective!

The Ants Go Marching by Mary Luders and Geoffrey Hayes (HarperFestival, 2000). A pull-the-flap version of the familiar song.

Silly Sounds Song
LANGUAGE ARTS

Silly Sound Off

Develop listening skills by having children create their own additional verses for the play. Have a child volunteer to make up a verse, using the sentence frame: "Have you ever heard a _____ go _____?" When the child is finished singing his or her riddle, the class answers just as the teacher in the play: "A _____ goes _____, not a _____!"

Literature Links

Barnyard Banter by Denise Fleming (Henry Holt & Co., 1994). Barnyard animals have some rhyming fun as each makes its own noise.

Buzz Said the Bee by Wendy Cheyette Lewison (Scholastic, 1992). Animals pile on top of one another as they make various sounds in this cumulative story.

Show and Tell
SOCIAL STUDIES

Reverse Show and Tell

Give "show and tell" time a new twist by having children switch roles! When a child brings something in for show and tell, have him or her show it to the group, but invite the rest of the group to tell about it, speculating and inferring information about the item. (A variation on this might be to have the group ask yes-or-no questions about the item the child has brought in and have the child answer.)

Literature Links

Show and Tell Day by Anne Rockwell and Lizzy Rockwell (HarperCollins, 2000). A kindergarten class experiences the fun of a favorite circle time activity.

Funny Fairy Tales

Literature Links

The Giant's Garden by Lisa Weedn Gilbert and Flavia Weedn (Hyperion, 1995). A grumpy giant bans children from his garden, but soon realizes that the plants are lonely without them!

Jack and the Beanstalk by Anthea Bell and Aljoscha Blau (North-South Books, 2000). A traditional retelling of the familiar tale.

Fee-Fi-Fo
LANGUAGE ARTS

Silly Seed Stories

Invite children to imagine how this play might be different if the giant had planted a seed other than a bean, such as an apple, pumpkin, or watermelon seed. Sit in a circle and begin a story (for instance, "The giant planted an apple seed in the ground..."). The child to your right continues the story, contributing the next sentence. Continue around the circle until you've created a complete silly seed story! You might wrap up by asking children to imagine different recipes Jack and the giant might have made at the end of the story with the different plants or fruits.

Literature Links

Goldilocks by Janice Russell (Boyd Mills Press, 1997). A traditional retelling.

Goldilocks and the Three Hares by Heidi Petach (Putnam, 1995). A parody of the classic tale, including mice, weasels, and hares!

Goldilocks and the Bears
LANGUAGE ARTS

Phonics Backpack

Fill a backpack with items whose names have the same beginning sound as *bear* (*baseball, button, beans, balloon, blue crayon, black crayon, small box, small paper or plastic bag*, and so on). Write the name of each item on an index card and place the cards in a pocket of the backpack. Invite pairs of children to lay out the cards and place each item on the matching card. Every several weeks, change the items in the backpack to include a different beginning sound.

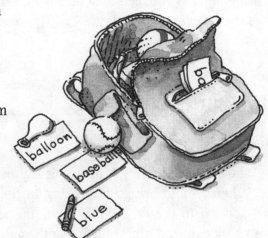

Three Little Pesky Pigs

DRAMATIC PLAY

What Happened First?

Have children each choose a different time of day and think of an activity the three pesky pigs might do at that time, such as 8:00–wake up, 8:30–eat breakfast, and so on. Show each time on a classroom display clock. Then choose two volunteers to come forward, share which time they chose, and act out the activities. The group decides which event of the two comes first in the day. Repeat with different pairs of children until everyone has had a turn.

Literature Links

The Three Little Pigs: An Old Story by Margaret Zemach (Farrar, Straus & Giroux, 1991). A traditional retelling.

Ziggy Piggy: And the Three Little Pigs by Frank Asch (Kids Can Press, 1998). A fourth pig is added in this cartoon spin on the traditional story.

Humpty Dumpty Mix-Up

LANGUAGE ARTS

Word Family Word Wall

Display the actual rhyme of Humpty Dumpty in a pocket chart or on chart paper and read together, pointing out that "wall" and "fall" are from the same word family. Make a word wall on the bulletin board to develop children's understanding of rhyme and word families:

☼ Make a large Humpty Dumpty by cutting an egg-shaped body from white paper. Give it a smiling face and accordion-folded strips of paper for arms and legs, and glue on hands and feet. Post Humpty Dumpty in the top center of the board.

☼ Give Humpty Dumpty a wall to sit on by placing 8-inch strips of paper underneath him across the board. Use the illustration as a guide. Write a word family ending on each strip of paper such as *-an*, *-op*, *-at*, or *-all*.

☼ Next to the bulletin board, hang a basket of pencils, glue sticks, and 4-by 8-inch paper "bricks." Invite students to visit the bulletin board to add bricks to Humpty Dumpty's wall. Students can write words from the different word families and add them to the wall under the corresponding word family ending.

Literature Links

Humpty Dumpty by Daniel Kirk (Putnam, 2000). A silly new twist on the familiar tale.

Humpty Dumpty by Kin Eagle and Rob Gilbert (Charlesbridge, 1999). A traditional retelling.

Literature Links

Animal Hide and Seek by Barbara Taylor and John Francis (Dorling Kindersley, 1998). Gorgeous "habitat" collages fill these pages, inviting children to find the animals within.

Goldfish Hide-and-Seek by Satoshi Kitamura (Farrar, Straus & Giroux, 1997). An underwater version of the familiar game!

Hide-and-Seek With Little Bo-Peep   MATH

Hide-and-Seek Sheep

Strengthen important math skills with this variation on hide-and-seek! Copy the sheep markers (below) so that each child will have at least ten. (You might copy more, depending on children's level.) Give each child a sheet of dark construction paper and ten sheep markers. Here's how to play:

☼ Help children pair off. The first player hides a certain number of sheep markers under the sheet of construction paper, placing the rest on his or her lap, out of the partner's sight. The second player guesses aloud how many sheep are hiding.

☼ The first player lifts up the sheet of construction paper, revealing the actual answer. If the second player guessed too *many*, that child gives the first player the number of markers to make up the difference. If he or she guessed too *few*, the first player gives the second player the number of markers to make up the difference. If the child guessed the *right number*, the second player wins all the sheep markers that were hidden and adds them to his or her pile.

☼ Children take turns until one player has all the markers.

EGG CRACK-UP

Mother Parrot
Giraffe 1
Giraffe 2

Scene 2

Giraffe 1: Look!
The eggs are shaking!

Giraffe 2: Oh, no!
Stop shaking, eggs!

4

Mother Parrot: Would you watch
the eggs in my nest?
I need to find some
nuts for breakfast.

Giraffe 1: We've never watched
eggs before.

Giraffe 2: What do we have
to do?

Mother Parrot: Just poke your necks
through these branches.
Then watch the eggs
in my nest.

Both Giraffes: Okay! We can do that.

Mother Parrot: Great! Good-bye!
I'm going to fly!

Scene 3

Mother Parrot: I'm back!

Giraffe 2: We're sorry! We didn't mean to let your eggs crack.

Mother Parrot: Don't be sorry! My baby parrots have hatched! Would you like to be my babysitters now?

Giraffe 2: Oh, no! Something is poking through the holes!

Giraffe 1: Look! Something is popping out!

Giraffe 2: Oh, no! What will Mother Parrot say?!

Giraffe 1: Look! We let her eggs crack!

Giraffe 1: We'd love to!

Giraffe 2: But baby parrots don't
crack, do they?

Mother Parrot: Of course not!
Only eggs do.

The End

Giraffe 1: Look!
The eggs are cracking!

Giraffe 2: Oh, no!
Stop cracking, eggs!

Giraffe 1: Look! Now there are
little holes in the eggs!

Mud! Mud! Mud!

★ Characters ★

Pigs 1 to 3

Pig Chorus 1 to 3

(Singing their lines to the tune of "Twinkle, Twinkle, Little Star")

Chickens

Ducks

Sheep

Chickens: Cluck! Cluck! Cluck!
Our feathers will get stuck!

4

Pig Chorus 1: Mud is squishy,
mud is fun!
Mud is great
for everyone.

Pig Chorus 2: Wiggle, giggle,
roll around.
Mud should cover
all the ground!

Pig Chorus 3: Mud is squishy,
mud is fun!
Mud is great
for everyone!

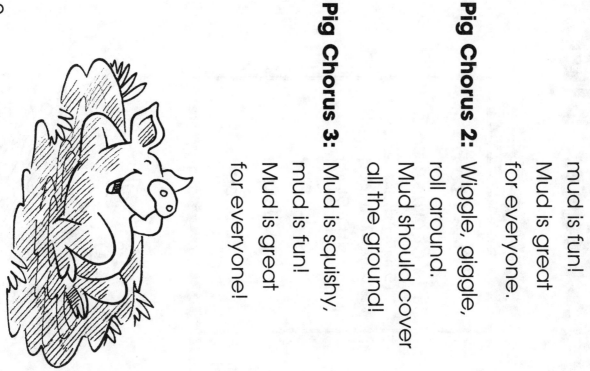

2

Pig 1: Let's ask our friends
to jump in the mud
with us!

Pig 2: Jump in, chickens,
ducks, and sheep!

Pig 3: The mud feels good.
It's not too deep!

3

Pig Chorus 1: Mud is squishy,
mud is fun!
Mud is great
for everyone.

Pig Chorus 2: Wiggle, giggle,
roll around.
Mud should cover
all the ground!

Pig Chorus 3: Mud is squishy,
mud is fun!
Mud is great
for everyone!

15 Easy-to-Read Mini-Book Plays Scholastic Professional Books

Sheep: Baaa! Baaa! Baaa!
Our wool will need a bath!

**Chickens,
Ducks, and
Sheep:** That's what YOU think!

The End

Ducks: Quack! Quack! Quack!
Ducks can't look like that!

5

Time to
Get Dressed

15 Easy-to-Read Mini-Book Plays   Scholastic Professional Books

★ **Characters** ★

Big Tree
Little Tree

Big Tree: Stop throwing your leaves
to the ground.
It's time to get dressed!

Little Tree: I won't get dressed!
I won't! I won't!

4

Big Tree: Some of your leaves are

on the ground.

Be a good little tree.

Pick them up and put them

back on your branches.

It's time to get dressed.

Little Tree: I don't want to get dressed!

15 Easy-to-Read Mini-Book Plays   Scholastic Professional Books

Big Tree: I'm the big tree.

You're the little tree.

Your branches are bare.

I'm telling you

it's time to get dressed.

Little Tree: I won't get dressed!

I won't! I won't!

Little Tree: But all the other trees have bare branches, too.

Big Tree: What are you talking about?

Big Tree: Little tree, look at yourself! All your pretty red, yellow, and brown leaves are on the ground. Your branches are bare!

Little Tree: Look around!
All the other trees
have dropped
their leaves, too!

Big Tree: Oh, I'm so-o-o-o sorry!
I forgot. It's fall!

The End

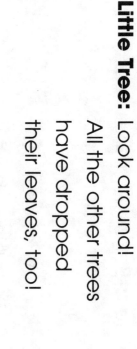

Big Tree: Stop this right now.
Stop throwing your leaves
to the ground!

Little Tree: I won't! I won't! I won't!

Lullaby for Bear

Bear
Snake
Skunk

Bear: Let me ask Skunk, too.

Hi, Skunk.

I can't go to sleep

for the winter

without a lullaby.

My mommy used to sing to me

before we would hibernate.

Skunk: Bear! It's warm and cozy

under my log.

I was almost asleep!

4

Bear: Hi, Snake.
Will you sing me a lullaby?
I can't go to sleep
for the winter
without a lullaby.
My mommy used to sing to me
before we would hibernate.

Snake: Bear! It's dark and quiet
under my rock.
I was almost asleep!

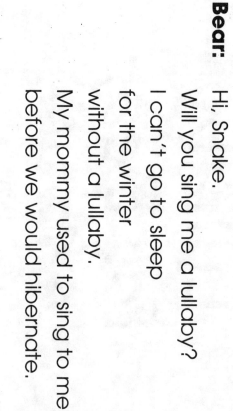

2

Bear: Sorry. But I need a lullaby.
Will you sing me to sleep?

Snake: Oh, all right.

3

Bear: Okay, Snake! Okay, Skunk!
I'm ready for you to
sing me to sleep.

**Snake
and
Skunk:** We can't believe
we're doing this!

(sing to the tune of "Rock-a-Bye-Baby")

Rock-a-bye Bear,
we'll sing you to sleep.
Close your brown eyes,
and don't make a peep.
Your soft bed of leaves
is cozy and warm.
We'll see you again
when winter is gone.

15 Easy-to-Read Mini-Book Plays   Scholastic Professional Books

Bear: <u>Zzzzzzzzz.</u>

Snake: Bear's asleep!

Skunk: Yawn!
Now I'm getting sleepy.

Snake: Yawn! Me, too.
That lullaby really works.

Skunk: Let's hurry back
to our cozy winter beds.

Snake: Time to hibernate!

Skunk: Goodnight, Snake!

Snake: Goodnight, Skunk!
See you in the spring!

The End

8

Bear: Sorry. But I need a lullaby.
Will you sing me to sleep?

Skunk: Oh, all right.

5

A Buzzy Day

(Sing to the tune of "London Bridge")

Flower Group

Bee Group

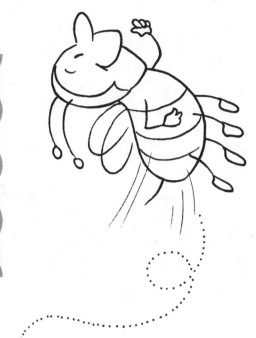

Bees: Goodbye flowers,
we are done.
Got our pollen,
on the run.
Thank you flowers,
it's been fun.
We'll buzz by later!
Buzzzzzzz!

The End

4

2

Flowers: We are flowers.
We're not trees.
We're not rocks.
We're not leaves.
We are waiting
for the bees.
Bees like our pollen!

Bees: We are busy, buzzing bees.
We're not bats.
We're not fleas.
May we have some
nectar, please
to make our honey?

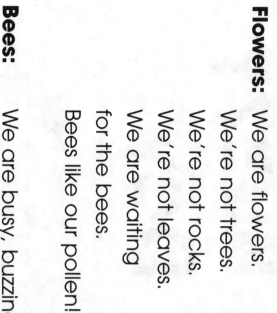

Flowers: Take some nectar,
busy bees.
Then drop some pollen,
won't you please?
Pollen helps us
make the seeds
for new flowers.

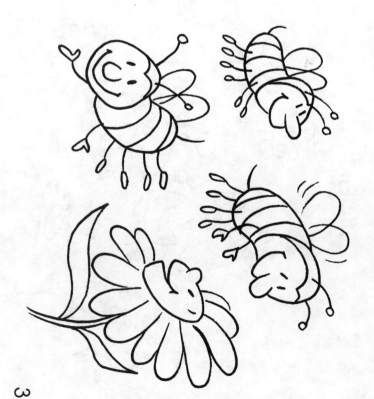

The Rainbow Zoo

★ Characters ★

Students 1 to 10

15 Easy-to-Read Mini-Book Plays   Scholastic Professional Books

Student 8: Another surprise was
a strange looking fellow.

Student 9: The zookeeper's toes
and nose
were bright yellow!

Student 10: We had quite a day!
We had fun.
Wouldn't you?

All: We'll always remember
the wild Rainbow Zoo!

The End

4

Student 1: Our class took a field trip
to the Rainbow Zoo.
When we walked
through the gate,
we saw something new!

Student 2: We saw five alligators,
but they weren't green.
They were the
brightest pink
we've ever seen!

2

Student 3: Purple camels
gave us a ride
past green-striped
elephants.

Student 4: Our eyes opened wide!

Student 5: The peacocks were white.

Student 6: The polar bears were red.

Student 7: And the big hippopotamus
had an orange head!

3

Monster Rules

15 Easy-to-Read Mini-Book Plays Scholastic Professional Books

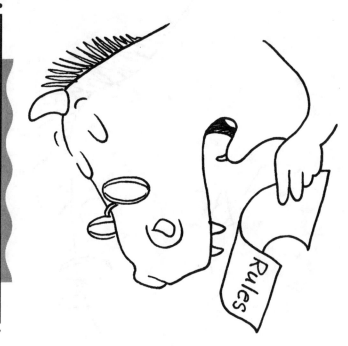

★ **Characters** ★

Teacher Monster

Student Monsters 1 to 3

Teacher Monster:
But you're monsters!

Well, okay, go ahead.

Try sharing,

but make scary faces!

All Student Monsters:
Hooray!

Little monsters can share!

ROAR!

4

**Teacher
Monster:** ROAR!
Good morning,
little monsters.
Are you ready to learn
the monster rules?

**All Student
Monsters:** ROAR!

15 Easy-to-Read Mini-Book Plays   Scholastic Professional Books

**Teacher
Monster:** Good!
Here is monster rule
number one.
Never share.

**Student
Monster 1:** May we try sharing
so we all get turns?

3

**Teacher
Monster:** Now for monster rule
number three.
Never be polite.
Little monsters never say
"please" or "thank you."

**Student
Monster 3:** May we try being polite?
It helps us make friends.

15 Easy-to-Read Mini-Book Plays   Scholastic Professional Books

**Teacher
Monster:** But you're monsters!
Well, okay,
go ahead and smile.
Good!
Your big monster teeth show.

**All Student
Monsters:** Hooray!
Little monsters can smile!
ROAR!

Teacher
Monster: Well, okay, be polite!

But please do it loudly
like monsters.

Oh, no! I said "please"!
I broke a monster rule!

The End

All Student
Monsters: Thank you! ROAR!

8

Teacher
Monster: Now for monster rule
number two.
Never smile.
Little monsters always frown.

Student
Monster 2: May we try smiling instead?
It feels good and
makes us happy.

5

100 Ants

★ Characters

Whole Class

Children 1 to 5

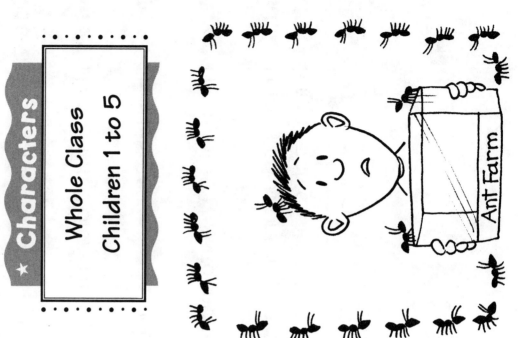

Ant Farm

Child 2: The ants must be hungry!
They're marching back,
arm in arm!

Child 3: They're hungry for cookies.

Child 4: Let's count as they come.

Child 5: . . . 98, 99, 100 ants are back
in their home.

Class: Hooray, hooray,
for 100 days!
We count to 100
in so many ways!

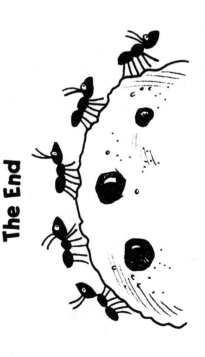

The End

4

Class: Hooray, hooray, for 100 days!
We count to 100
in so many ways!

Child 1: I brought 100 cookies to eat.

Child 2: I brought 100 drums to beat.

Child 3: I brought 100 shoes to wear.

Child 4: I brought 100 toys to share.

Child 5: I brought 100 ants to show.
But my ant farm is empty!
Where did they go?

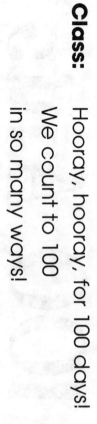

2

Child 1: Look! Those ants
are everywhere!

Child 2: Ants on my nose!

Child 3: Ants on the chairs!

Child 4: Black ants marching.
100 ants!

Child 5: Ants in our socks
and ants in our pants!

Child 1: Here are some cookies
to put in your farm.

3

Silly Sounds Song

Students: Have you ever heard
a monkey
go meow-meow
and meow-meow?
Have you ever heard
a monkey
go meow-meow-
meow-meow?

Teacher: A cat goes meow,
not a monkey!

Students: We know!
We just wanted to see
if you were listening!

The End

4

Teacher: It's time to practice
your animal sounds song.
Ready? Sing!

Students: Have you ever heard
an elephant
go moo-moo and
moo-moo?
Have you ever heard
an elephant
go moo-moo-moo-moo?

Teacher: A cow goes moo,
not an elephant!

Moo!

2

Students: Have you ever heard a lion
go quack-quack and
quack-quack?
Have you ever heard a lion
go quack-quack-
quack-quack?

Teacher: A duck goes quack,
not a lion!

Students: Have you ever heard
a chicken
go ruff-ruff and ruff-ruff?
Have you ever heard
a chicken
go ruff-ruff-ruff-ruff?

Teacher: A dog goes ruff,
not a chicken!

3

Show and Tell

Child 2:   Is Binky under a desk?
He likes to crawl.

**First
Grade Class:** E-e-e-e-k!

4

Child 1: For show and tell
I brought my
5 pet worms.
1-2-3-4-5.
In this cup are
Slim, Swim, Jim, Tim,
and Kim.

First Grade Class: Wow! Worms!

2

Child 2: I brought my
5 pet snakes.
1-2-3-4-5.
In this cage are
Slinky, Dinky, Pinky,
Stinky, and . . .
Oh, no! Where's Binky?
Binky got out!

First Grade Class: E-e-e-e-k! SNAKES!

3

Second Grade Class: E-e-e-e-k!

Child 1: Why is the class next door screaming?

15 Easy-to-Read Mini-Book Plays Scholastic Professional Books

Child 2: Is Binky on the teacher's desk? He likes to look for things to eat.

Child 2: They found Binky!

The End

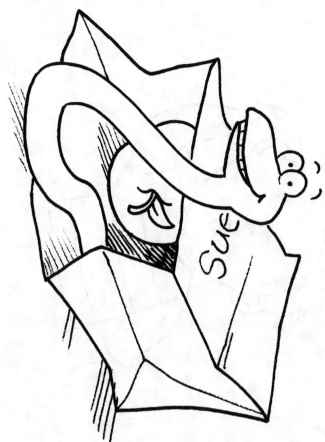

8

Child 2: Is Binky in the sink?
He likes water to drink.

**First
Grade Class:** E-e-e-ek!

5

Fee-Fi-Fi-Fo

Jack

Giant

Jack: A giant?
I'm climbing higher to see!

Giant: Fee-fi-boo-hoo!
I'm afraid. What will I do?

4

Jack: Wow! The beans I planted
sure do grow!
I'll climb this beanstalk.
Up, up, up I go!

Giant: Fee-fi-fo-fum.
I'm stuck up here,
and it sure isn't fun!

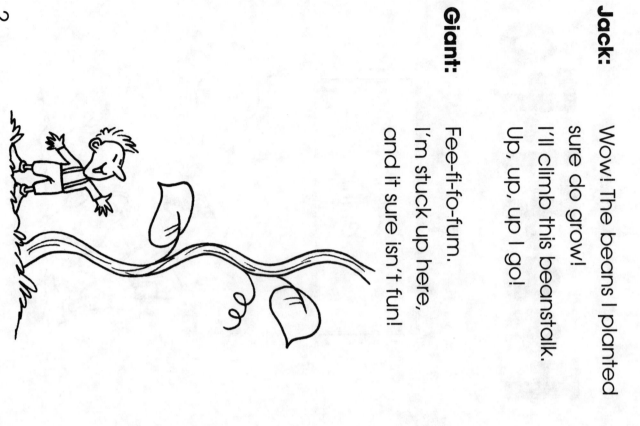

2

Jack: Who was that?

Giant: Fee-fi-fo-frown.
It's the giant.
I'm afraid to climb down.

3

Jack: How did you end up
on this beanstalk, anyway?

Giant: I thought I wanted
some beans for lunch.
While I climbed up,
it grew a whole bunch.

Jack: You're doing great!

Giant: Fee-fi-fo-glad!
You're the best friend
I ever had!

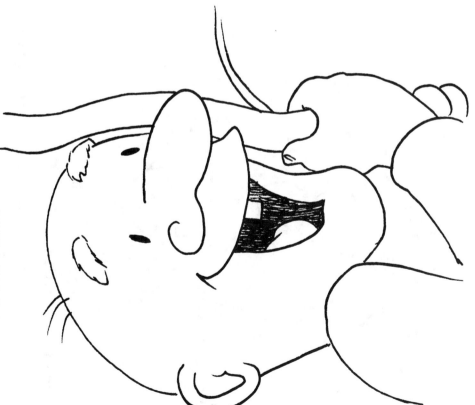

Jack: We got down the beanstalk.
I'm glad I helped you.
Now we are safe.
Let's cook a bean stew!

**Giant
and Jack:** Fee-fi-fo-YUM!

The End

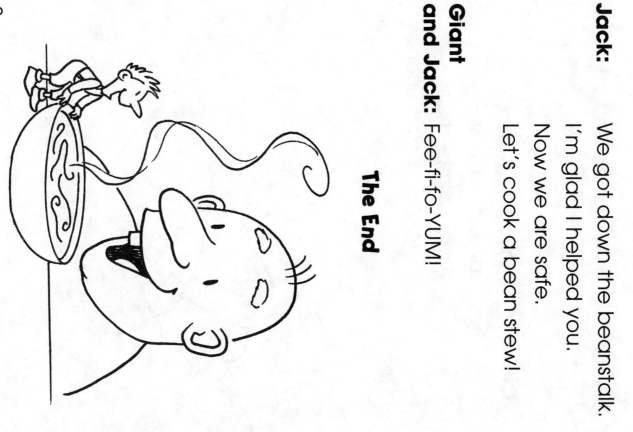

15 Easy-to-Read Mini-Book Plays Scholastic Professional Books

Jack: Don't worry, giant,
and don't move around.
I'll come up to get you,
we'll slide to the ground.

Giant: Fee-fi-oh-no!
There's a thousand feet
still left to go!

Goldilocks and the Bears

Goldilocks: Oh, no! Brown bears
are everywhere!
They're running races
down the hall.
They're jumping
on the beds!
They're bouncing
big beach balls!

Brown Bears: Boing! Boing! Boing!

Goldilocks: Hi, Baby Bear!
Come in, come in!

Baby Bear: May my friends
come in, too?

Goldilocks: Sure!

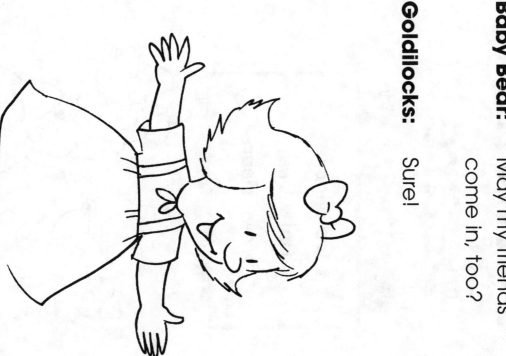

2

Baby Bear: Gr-r-reat!
Did you hear that,
brown bears?
You can play
in Goldilocks' house, too!

Brown Bears: Here we come!

3

Baby Bear: Bye, bears!
           Bye, Goldilocks!

Goldilocks: Next time I'll come
           to your house to play.

7

Baby Bear: Here come more
           brown bears!

Goldilocks: Oh, no!
           Brown bears
           are everywhere!
           They're riding bikes
           across the floor.
           They're riding through
           the bedrooms!
           They're riding out
           the door!

Brown Bears: Beep! Beep! Beep!

6

8

Baby Bear: Gr-r-reat!
But don't come
at breakfast.
We'll be out for a walk.

The End

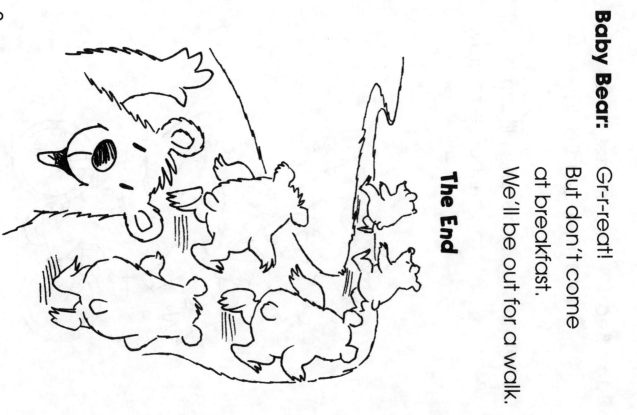

Baby Bear: Here come more
brown bears!

Goldilocks: Oh, no! Brown bears
are everywhere!
They're in my baby
brother's crib.
They're drinking
baby bottles!
And they're wearing
baby bibs!

Brown Bears: Burp!

5

Three Little Pesky Pigs

Pesky Pigs 1 to 3

Wolf

All Pesky Pigs: Knock! Knock! Knock!

Big, Bad Wolf!

Big, Bad Wolf!

Let us come in!

We're the

Three Pesky Pigs.

Pesky Pig 1: I need to borrow

some sugar.

Pesky Pig 2: I need to borrow

some soap.

Pesky Pig 3: I need to borrow

some milk.

4

Pesky Pig 1: It's midnight and
I'm hungry.
I'll bake sugar cookies.
I'll borrow some sugar
from Wolf.

Pesky Pig 2: I can't sleep.
I'll wash my dirty clothes.
I'll borrow some soap
from Wolf.

Pesky Pig 3: I can't sleep.
I'll make a cup
of warm milk.
I'll borrow some milk
from Wolf.

2

Pesky Pig 1: It takes one hour
to walk to Wolf's house.

Pesky Pig 2: We'll be there
at one o'clock
in the morning.

Pesky Pig 3: It's one o'clock.
Here we are!

3

Pesky Pig 1: Now it's six o'clock
in the morning.
Let's take our things
to Wolf.

Pesky Pig 2: It will take us one hour
to walk there.

Pesky Pig 3: It's seven o'clock
in the morning.
Here we are.

**All Pesky
Pigs:** Knock! Knock! Knock!
Big, Bad Wolf!
Big, Bad Wolf!
Let us come in!
We're the
Three Pesky Pigs.

Pesky Pig 1: If you give me
some sugar,
I'll bring you
sugar cookies.

Pesky Pig 2: If you give me
some soap,
I'll wash your
dirty clothes.

Pesky Pig 3: If you give me
some milk,
I'll bring you
some warm milk.

Wolf: All right. Here you are.
Now let me sleep!

8

Wolf: Snore! Snore! Snore!

Pesky Pig 1: Listen!
He's sound asleep.

Pesky Pig 2: We'll just have to
come back later.

Pesky Pig 3: Right! When we have
trouble sleeping!

The End

ZZZZZ

Wolf: What do you think
this is? A store?
Not by the hair on
my chinny-chin-chin!
Go away and
let me sleep!

Humpty Dumpty Mix-Up

15 Easy-to-Read Mini-Book Plays Scholastic Professional Books

Children 1 to 5

Child 1: Wait! Can't anyone get this right?

Children 2 to 5: Humpty Dumpty sat on a wall.
Humpty Dumpty had a great fall.
Humpty Dumpty yelled, "Whee! This is neat!"
For Humpty Dumpty wore springs on his feet!

Child 1: I GIVE UP!

The End

4

Child 1: Can someone tell me
how Humpty Dumpty goes?

Child 2: Sure! Humpty Dumpty
sat on a horse.
Humpty Dumpty said,
"Giddy-up!" of course.

Child 1: Wait! That's not how it goes.

Child 3: Let me try. Humpty Dumpty
sat on a tack.
Humpty Dumpty
heard himself crack!

2

Child 1: No! That's not how it goes!

Child 4: Let me try.
Humpty Dumpty
sat on a cake.
Humpty Dumpty
made a mistake!

Child 1: Hey! That's not how it goes!

Child 5: Let me try. Humpty Dumpty
sat on a boat.
Humpty Dumpty
hoped he would float.

3

Hide-and-Seek With Little Bo-Peep

Sheep 4:   Okay.
But I don't want to play.
I'm hungry!

Sheep 3:   Now I'm hungry, too.
I want to eat hay.

4

Sheep 1: Let's play Hide-and-Seek!

Sheep 2: We'll hide from
Little Bo-Peep!

Sheep 3: She'll never find us!

2

Sheep 4: I don't want to play.
I'm hungry.

Sheep 1: Sh-h-h! She'll hear you.

Sheep 2: Let's hide in this wagon.

3

Farmer: Don't worry.
Here's some hay.
They'll be back
when they get hungry.

**Sheep
2 to 4:** Oh boy! Hay!
We don't want
to play anymore.

Farmer: Hi, Little Bo-Peep.
Where are your sheep?

Bo-Peep: They're lost!
I can't find them anywhere!

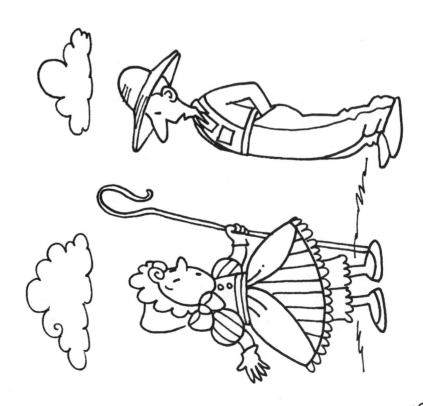

Sheep 1: Okay. Now I'm hungry, too.
Let's go eat!

All Sheep: Hi, Little Bo-Peep.
We're ba-a-ack!

The End

8

Sheep 1: Quiet! Stay down low.
She'll never find us
here in the wagon.

Sheep 4: Okay. But I'm hungry.

Sheep 3: Me, too.

Sheep 2: Now I'm hungry, too.

Sheep 1: Sh-h-h!
Here she comes
with the farmer!

5